The Ultimate Goodreads Guide for Authors

By

Barb Drozdowich

Babs Hightower

Copyright

Introduction

Welcome to The *Ultimate Goodreads Guide for Authors*. Although much has been written on the Goodreads website, in blog posts and other publications, the authors, Barb Drozdowich and Babs Hightower, wanted to compile a comprehensive guide for the writer that left no stone unturned.

Goodreads is *the* candy store for readers. It has been described as the place where insatiable readers, book bloggers and book buyers hang out. The website has more than 21 million registered users and almost all of its features are completely free. What better place to interact with the potential readers of your books than this reader heaven?

To introduce the authors of this book, Barb Drozdowich is a multi-published author, who works with writers on a daily basis, helping them to understand blogging through Wordpress coaching and showing them how to create a winning Author Platform.

Babs Hightower works in PR, holding the roles of publicity director over the Scandalous Imprint at Entangled Publishing and publicity director at World Castle Publishing. She also performs a lot of freelance work for several clients, assisting them with the promotional side of the book business. She recently published a PR book to help authors. Lastly, Babs is a Goodreads Librarian and brings her specialized inside knowledge to this book.

Barb and Babs met through their blogs, which have romance in common. Barb owns Sugarbeat's Books and prefers regency romance while Babs owns Babs Book Bistro and favors western romance.

Babs and Barb both feel that Goodreads is frequently an underused part of an Author's Platform. In our work, we hear complaints that range from it not being intuitive enough, to authors being apprehensive of the bad behavior they encounter on the site to a simple lack of understanding of the features it offers authors.

We feel that Goodreads has a lot of under utilized gems of marketing opportunities and we hope that this book helps you better understand the value of including Goodreads as part of your Author Platform.

According to Bestselling Author, Jonathan Gunson, there are "more than 20 million reviews written on Goodreads. Members have added more than 210 million books to their online 'bookshelves' and they have added 640,000 books to Lists." As part of his article (Why Every Author Must Be on Goodreads in 2013) he includes the above information and more in a wonderful infographic.

It is generally accepted that Goodreads is an impartial player in the book-marketing world. In an article in The New York Times, Leslie Kaufman tells us that Goodreads is host to about 20,000 organically occurring online book clubs for every preference. Ms Kaufman quotes another New York Times article "The Best Book Reviews Money Can Buy" by David Streitfeld that says "Amazon has lost some trust among readers recently amid concerns that its reviews and recommendations can contain hidden agendas." Leslie Kaufman then goes on to quote Amanda Close, who runs the digital marketplace for Random House. She says "Because Goodreads is not a publisher or retailer, people feel that the information is not getting manipulated. People trust them because they are so crowd-sourced and their members are fanatics. You can't buy a five-star review there."

Goodreads allows members to create a personal account, list books, assign them to shelves, join groups and participate in events and giveaways. They use the book information that members add to make recommendations of what to read next.

Goodreads also offers special accounts for authors. They allow authors to list their books, upload excerpts, host giveaways, make friends and fans and even hook up their blog feed so that their fans can keep up to date. When talking about Goodreads, we often emphasize the number of readers with an account, but keep in mind that somewhere in the region of 75,000 authors hold one too.

When creating your Author Platform, Goodreads should play a significant part. You could spend all day chatting to people on social networks such as Facebook, and Twitter, but only on Goodreads can you be certain that everyone is a reader. That being said, in common with Facebook and Twitter, asking everyone who looks in your direction to read your book is not polite. It is unacceptable and considered spam. Instead, join the community and participate. Be a reader first; then be an author.

Chapter 1— Create a Personal Profile

The starting point of creating a presence on Goodreads is to open an account, and the website offers two types. Readers can set up a Personal Profile while authors can set up an Author Profile. Anyone joining Goodreads must start with a Personal Profile and then they can add an Author Profile, if applicable.

Although setting up a Goodreads account is fairly straightforward, it is really important to be as complete as possible in the information you provide.

Basic Application

First, we will walk you through the process of setting up a Personal Profile from the very beginning.

The initial step, as you can see from the graphic above, is to create a free account, starting with your name, email address and password, as indicated by the arrows. Please note that you can also sign in using Facebook, Twitter or your Google identity (indicated by the lower arrow). Although you are welcome to enter your credentials, it is faster and easier to create your account via Facebook. That way, when you open one of these websites, your browser will automatically log you in to the other.

Once you click on 'Sign up,' an email will be sent to the email address you provided (or your Facebook email), asking you to confirm your account.

Once you have confirmed it, you will see the above graphic on the website. The arrow on the left-hand side points to the statement indicating that your email address has been verified. You will notice that you can then invite people from various sources to join you on Goodreads. There is a choice of Facebook, Twitter, Yahoo Mail or Gmail, or, as the right-hand arrow indicates, entering email addresses individually. Although it is not indicated on this screen, you are presented with the option of skipping this step. However, you are ultimately on Goodreads to network, so you should put an effort into finding friends at some point!

The next step is to choose your favorite genres. As the graphic above indicates, Goodreads will use your choices to make better book recommendations to you and customize your browsing experience. Choose carefully.

Once you have finished, click 'Continue' and you will be presented with the above screen. This is where you start rating books. We would strongly suggest that you rate some titles, or else indicate a few that you are interested in reading. In common with other social media, Goodreads is a place to interact and socialize. We are all readers on Goodreads. You may also be an author, but you are a reader first. We are suspicious of people who want to friend us and have not indicated any books. We will come back to this point when we talk about shelves, but for now, rating books and indicating the ones you wish to read is part of the social aspect of Goodreads.

Once you have indicated several books, click on 'See Your Recommendations' and the following screen will appear:

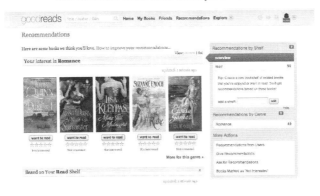

You will notice that we have indicated an interest in several romance novels, and Goodreads has supplied us with some suggestions of what to read next. At this point you can create a shelf, and add all or some of these books to it. Although shelves will be discussed in more detail below, your Goodreads profile comes with some preset 'shelves' that you can assign books to. They include, Read, To-Read, and Currently Reading.

Once you have spent enough time on this step, create a shelf, add a few of the recommended books to it, and move on.

Next, click on 'Home' on the upper menu bar and the following screen will pop up:

Goodreads will encourage you to post information to your Facebook Timeline, as well as connecting your profile to your Twitter account. Again, this is a social media network, and there is no harm in sharing information from your Goodreads profile on your Facebook Timeline. We would therefore suggest you click on 'Add Goodreads to My Timeline' and follow the steps to do so. If you are strongly opposed to doing this, then click on 'X' to skip it. This will be discussed again, when we get to the Apps section.

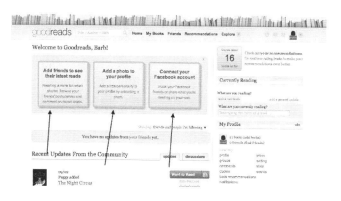

Once you get rid of the Facebook screen, the Goodreads homepage will appear. Initially, you will be encouraged to do a number of things. The choices that you can see in the graphic above, indicated by the arrows, are:

- Add friends to see their latest reads
- Add a photo to your Goodreads Profile
- Connect your Facebook account

Chapter 2 — Personal Profile Tab

Set up your Personal Profile next, so that people will be able to find you. Be as thorough as possible when providing your details.

Click the "Add photo to your profile' box. This will bring up your 'My Account' page. Along the top of this section is a line of tabs (indicated by an arrow), showing your profile, settings, emails, feeds, etc. We will deal with all of these tabs before leaving this section. Do you *have* to fill out all this information? No, but the majority of it is important in one way or another, so you might as well deal with it straight away.

We will start with your profile tab as seen in the graphic above. Fill out your first name and last name (author name). Make sure your last name is visible by any one, because this is important for search engines. As an author, you are a public figure, and you do not want to do anything that will interfere with the search engines finding you on your various platforms. Create a user name that combines your first and last name as an author (if possible). This will create a custom URL for your Goodreads Profile. Barb's full name is Barb Drozdowich, which makes her custom URL http://goodreads.com/barbdrozdowich. This is easy to remember and view.

State/Province Code

BC

Country

Canada

Location Viewable By:

friends only

Date of Birth

Age & Birthday Privacy:

Age to Goodreads members, Birthday to friends

My Web Site (e.g. http://www.myblog.com)

http://www.sugarbeatsbooks.com

My Interests — favorite subjects, or really anything you know a lot about
(in comma separated phrases, please)

What Kind of Books Do You Like to Read?

Romance

About Me (tips) ◀——————

```
Social Media and Wordpress Consultant Barb Drozdowich has
taught at Colleges, trained technical personnel in the banking
industry and, most recently, used her expertise to help
hundreds of authors develop the social media platform needed
to succeed in today's fast evolving publishing world. She owns
Bakerview Consulting and manages the popular blog, Sugarbeat's
Books.
```

If you don't want anyone to know your birthday or your age, you can choose the 'Age & Birthday to no one' choice from the drop-down menu. Fill in your website/blog address, complete with http://, and a few words about your interests. Make sure you indicate what type of books you like to read, and include a short biography at the bottom (this can be your official author biography). If you click on the 'Tips' prompt (see black arrow in graphic above), there is some help available. Unlike other areas, you can enter clickable links here. If you do not know how to do this, use the information in the tips area to help you. Since you are a member of Goodreads, partly to network with others, make sure there is a clickable link to your website or blog for readers to find you easily.

Once you have finished, click on 'save profile settings.'

The last step is to upload your author photo in the upper right of this page.

This is a necessary step for any author. You need a photograph that shows a clear view of your face. As you can see from the graphic above, you can actually upload more than one image if you want. Your initial one will be your official author photograph.

Chapter 3 — Settings Tab

This section/tab is a collection of various things that most people ignore. Goodreads sends out a lot of notifications and if don't want your inbox filled, please look through this information carefully and choose what you receive wisely. We will help with some suggestions.

At the top of the page (see graphic above), you will notice your email address and password (encoded). This is where you can change them, if necessary. We suggest you leave the default settings in place for who can view your reviews, but possibly restrict who can send you a private message or an email. You will notice that Goodreads currently shares book reviews with Sony, Alibris, Stanza, WorldCat, Powell's Books, Blio, BetterWorldBooks, the LA Public Library, Edelweiss, USA Today, Kobo and Lexcycle, and I'm sure this list will expand as time passes. This is both good and bad. If your book has a lot of 5-star reviews, these might be displayed on book buying sites, but the 1-star reviews might appear too.

Lastly, you have the ability to issue a challenge question to potential friends. As an author, you are trying to use this site to network and make as many friends as possible, so we'd suggest not setting a question.

Chapter 4 — Emails Tab

On the emails page/tab, you have the ability to limit the number of notifications that are sent to your inbox. You will probably get a huge amount, so the idea of encouraging more is overwhelming. Make your choices carefully. If you are not planning to check Goodreads on a regular basis, you will need to keep track of what is happening there.

Chapter 5 — Feeds Tab

This page will allow you to include or exclude various pieces of information on your Update Feed. Many don't understand what an Update Feed is, so we'll explain. To find your Update Feed, click on the home button on the menu bar and you will see your version of the graphic below.

As you can see in the above graphic, the title of this screen is 'Recent Updates' and it has two parts. The view in the graphic above is the 'updates' part of this view. Here you can view what your friends have been up to. Have they entered giveaways, friended someone new, added a book to a shelf, or left a comment on a review?

The second part of the screen is the 'discussions' view as seen below:

19

The 'discussions' view keeps you up to date on what has been posted in the various groups you belong to, and other discussions you have been part of.

If you have a look at the 'feeds' tab (in the graphic below) you will see that you have control over whether this information appears or not.

If you take a look through the list above, you will see that a lot of this has to do with networking. You can share with your friends what you have done recently on the site. Did you answer a poll, vote for a video or respond to an event? Since none of these things end up as emails in our inboxes, we generally don't uncheck any of them. That might not be your opinion, however. Examine the list and uncheck the items you don't want shared on the 'Feed'.

The next section/tab to look at is the Apps tab.

Chapter 6 - Apps Tab

As its name suggests, this page deals with Goodreads Apps.

If you haven't done so already, you can connect your Facebook and Twitter accounts to Goodreads. This will make networking easier. Every time you rate a book or add one to a shelf, or update your reading status, for example, this information will be posted to your Facebook Timeline. The same option exists for Twitter – by hooking up your profile to your Goodreads account, your various activities will be tweeted automatically.

You can let Goodreads know what type of e-reader you have, or choose to post your Goodreads reviews to your blog on WordPress or Blogger. We don't like to do this, as we prefer to post them directly, but the choice is yours – the ability is there.

Mobile App

One-fifth of the site's account holders use this app and you know this number will only increase, so you need to be familiar with what your readers have access to.

We both use an iPhone and have installed the app. It is also available for Android and other smart phones as well.

Click on the mobile app that matches your phone, and you will find it easy to set up and use. It is an uncomplicated way for you to keep up with your readers and fans, and to take a virtual shopping list to the used bookstore. Below are two screenshots showing how the app looks on an iPhone.

As you can see from these screenshots, you can do anything on the app that you can do on the Goodreads page itself.

Chapter 7 —Widgets Tab

This tab/page allows you to create widgets for your blog to show off your activities, including what you are reading and the groups you belong to. They are an important networking tool between you and your readers. Once your choices have been made, the code is provided for you to place on the sidebar of your blog. Please note: these widgets will not display on free Wordpress blogs.

Won't work on sites that don't allow JavaScript widgets.

In the graphic above, you can see a widget that was created for Barb's blog's sidebar, showing three books on her 'Read' bookshelf. The code that we need to display this widget is provided in the lower right of the graphic. (Indicated by an arrow) and it can be copied and pasted into a sidebar widget as can be seen in the following graphics:

The graphic above shows the code from Goodreads pasted into a Text widget on a Wordpress blog. Click on the blue 'Save' button and you will see the following on your sidebar:

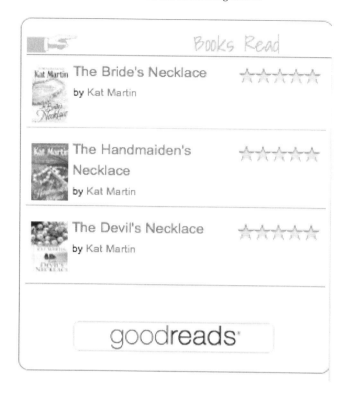

Grid Widget

A fits-anywhere, variable width widget that shows a cool-looking grid of your books. Fully configurable.
Won't work on sites that don't allow JavaScript widgets.

Our favorite is the Grid Widget (see above). It displays books by cover art, either in small or medium size (shown above). As we did with the previous widget, copy the code in the box indicated by the arrow above, and paste into a text widget and display on a sidebar. (see graphic below)

Barb's to-read book montage

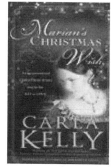
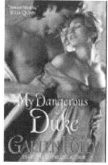

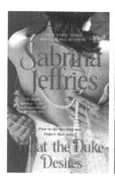

Chapter 8 — Book Links

The last two tabs on the 'My Profile' page are 'Book Links' and 'Purchases'. You can see the 'Book Links' page below. You can personalize which 'buy' links appear with the books you look at. We like to customize ours, so that we are not presented with a whole bunch of 'buy' links that we will never use. The Purchases page will list the items you bought through Goodreads. Yes, it is possible to purchase a book while browsing!

Check Your Progress

Lastly, you need to check your Personal Profile to make sure everything is correct. You can do this by clicking on the 'See my Profile' link in the upper right-hand corner (see graphic above). This will enable you to see it in the same way, as everyone else will. Viewing your profile like this gives you the opportunity to proofread your work. To view the progress that we have made on Barb's profile, view the graphic below. The upper arrow indicates the direct URL for her personal account. When you are adding a Goodreads 'Follow' icon to your blog, this is where you will find the URL to use.

Chapter 9 — Friends versus Fans

In the upper section of the above graphic, the number of friends you have is indicated. This will be our next job – finding friends. Clicking on the 'More Friends' link at the bottom of the graphic and you will be taken to the following page:

You would have seen this page right at the beginning of the sign-up process. If you have not already found friends via Facebook, Twitter and your email (if you have Gmail or Yahoo Mail), we encourage you to do so. Remember, Goodreads is supposed to be a social network. One of the things that we will encourage you to do is to make friends and acquire fans. There is a lot of emphasis on acquiring friends on Goodreads. Much is written about it. As an author, fans are almost more important in our opinion.

So, let's define friends and fans:

- A friend is a two-way commitment: both people have to agree to it. If you are friends with someone, their reviews and comments will appear in your 'Recent Updates' or what we refer to as 'feed', and yours in theirs.

- Being a fan is a one-way activity: a reader can become a fan of yours, but you are not required to do anything. You don't have to accept or approve them, or interact. If someone is a fan of an author, that author's blog posts, reviews and comments will appear in their feed, but their own comments and reviews will not necessarily appear in the author's feed, unless the author and the user are also friends.

- It is possible to be both a fan and a friend.

In terms of networking potential, what is better than a large number of people being notified by email that you have created a new blog post? Those people who have not subscribed to your blog will receive your posts just because they are your fans on Goodreads.

Once you have acquired a collection of friends, your 'Friends' page will look like this:

Friends are listed on the left-hand side, along with the book they are currently reading or any status update they have put in place. This list can be viewed alphabetically by first name, not surname, using the row of letters along the top. It can also be sorted using a number of criteria, as you can see in the drop-down in the graphic below.

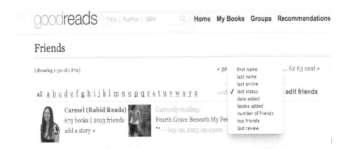

Lastly, it is possible to edit friends. Once you click on the 'Edit Friends' link, each entry will show an 'X' beside it, allowing you to remove someone from the list. The person will not be notified.

There is a limit on the number of friends you can acquire – 5,000. Since you are limited in number, focus your attention on readers and don't fill your ranks with fellow authors. Although they are likely to be very supportive of you, you really want to be using Goodreads to network with potential readers of your books.

Chapter 10 — Organizing Books

Remember, Goodreads is a site for readers! You will need to participate on the site as a reader first and an author second. Joining the website with the sole purpose of spamming people with 'buy my books' links will not be appreciated.

Create Shelves of Books

Goodreads allows every member with a Personal Profile to create virtual shelves for their books. There are default shelves that every account comes with – Read, To-Read and Currently Reading. One of the activities that you were encouraged you to do during the initial steps of creating an account was to list some books. Either list them from the books that you have read, all time favorites, maybe, or books that you are interested in reading in the future.

We are suspicious of people who want to friend us if they have no books listed as part of their Profile. (or only one book – theirs) Goodreads is supposed to be a reader site. You are a reader, so participate as one and add some titles. As we have mentioned before, 21 millions readers are members on Goodreads. Take some time to share with others what books you like.

We like the ability to add books to our virtual shelves. Barb used to go into her local used bookstore or library armed with a binder full of paper lists of books that she had read and those she wanted to read. Now that she has the Goodreads mobile app on her phone, she only needs to take that shopping. The "to buy" shelf on her mobile app doesn't take up nearly as much space as that binder of paper!

As soon as a book is put on a shelf it appears in your the newsfeed. (remember the Recent Updates section from above?) You *want* your books to be listed as 'To Read' or 'Currently Reading' by Goodreads members, or in other words, you want your books to be placed on other's 'to-read' and 'currently reading' shelves. On Goodreads, this is more important than your book being reviewed or receiving stars (in contrast to Amazon where a review is the vital thing). The Goodreads algorithm pays attention to how many times your book is placed on shelves. Authors would like readers to mark their book as 'Want to read' for a purpose. The more your book shows up on the 'Want to Read' shelves, the higher it will show on the 'Popular Books' or 'I Want to Read' lists. We'll discuss lists later.

To see the books that you have entered, click on 'My Books' link on the top menu bar, indicated by the top arrow in the graphic below.

Let's assume you have added some books; now you can sort them onto shelves. Goodreads provides you with some preset ones: Read, Currently-Reading and To-Read. Although you can use the preset shelves, we recommend creating some custom ones using the 'Add Shelf' link (see left-hand arrow).

Let's look at the right side of the graphic above. Each book entry has a cover image, title, author, average rating, the rating you gave it (if you rated it), the shelf it belongs on, the date you read it (if you provided that information) and the date you added it to your profile. You also have the ability to edit or view the entry, as well as clicking an 'X' to delete it.

In the line above the book listings, you will see the 'add books' link. If you click this, the following screen will appear:

This screen will allow you to search a book by title, author or ISBN. To demonstrate, we entered the name of one of our favorite authors, clicked 'Search' and received the following:

You can see from the graphic above that if you hover over the end of the 'Want to Read' button, you will be presented with a choice of shelves on which to place the book. If none of these shelves is appropriate, you can create a new one on the spot.

It is possible to change how your collection of books is viewed. The arrows in the graphic above indicate where you can switch back and forth between Cover and Table view. This screenshot shows the 'Table' view. The arrow on the right shows you the Print option. A note of warning: if you have listed a lot of books, this function will only print what you can see on screen, potentially printing out a large number of pages.

Because of the website's algorithms, the number of reviews, comments and times readers place your book on the 'Want to Read' shelf are highly important. Let's talk about each one separately.

Chapter 11 — Reviews

Many regard reviews on Goodreads as better than those posted anywhere else. Goodreads is a free community site for readers, which lets members rate and review books. For the most part, Goodreads' reviewers do not care if you buy, borrow or ignore the book, because they just enjoy reading and sharing their thoughts.

Sorting Reviews

Reviews can be sorted according to various criteria. Although Goodreads encourages you to read your friends' reviews first, if you scroll down you will find a section labeled 'Community Reviews' listing them all (see graphic below).

There are two ways of sorting the reviews for a book. As you can see from the graphic above, they can be filtered by:

- Number of stars
- Edition numbers

Although you can filter, which reviews you see, they can also be sorted by a number of criteria, as you can see from the graphic above. If you are regularly reading the reviews for a particular book, you might want to sort them from newest to oldest, so you are only reading the newest ones that have been added.

Lastly, a summary of the ratings can be viewed by clicking on 'rating details.' As you can see in the graphic above, the book that we were looking at had 6885 five star reviews or 39% of the reviews were 5 star. You can also see that 38721 people have added this book on their to-read shelf! This is an interesting little snapshot of the results that a book has garnered.

Search for your favorite book and play with the sorting system. Become familiar with it.

One last comment about reviews: the only possible response to a bad one is 'Thank you for reading my book.' There is absolutely nothing to be gained from going after the reviewer on any forum, be it Goodreads or Amazon, or somewhere else. You should not retaliate under any circumstances.

Stars

Goodreads has a star rating system; there are five stars to use, with one being the lowest and five the highest. It is always best to read the reviews (not just look at the stars), because some people will give half stars and explain why. From our point of view, the comments are far more important.

Chapter 12 — Comments

Comments can be left almost anywhere on Goodreads. It is possible to leave your opinion everywhere it seems. Let's talk about some of the places that you will find comments.

Goodreads gives you the opportunity to comment on reviews.

In the above graphic you can see the review for a book, the number of 'likes' this review got, and the fact that it got 10 comments. It is possible to click on 'view all 10 comments' and see all the comments posted.

Comments can be left on a blog post as you can see below:

The arrow above shows that there are 2 comments on this blog post.

It is possible to search for your own comments. Go to your Homepage, and find your avatar on the far right. Click on your avatar and you will bring up a summary of your profile.

From there you see all the comments that have been left for you.

If you click on 'Home' on the top menu bar you will be brought to your home screen. Scroll down and on the right you will find a box like in the graphic below:

The arrow points at the word comment. If you click on this link, you will be brought to a summary screen as you see below:

This area, labeled 'My Recent Posts,' is a summary of your recent comment activity. As you can see it shows a variety of information.

Remember to treat other readers, as you would like to be treated yourself. Leaving thoughtless comments is not appreciated and may result in an unnecessary flame war.

Tags and Keywords

Tags and Keywords are used liberally on Goodreads. Generally speaking, tags are single words or short phrases that are used to describe something. When creating your blog posts you can think of tags as similar to the index of a book. For example, if we were entering a quiz about one of our favorite regency romance books, The Duke & I by Julia Quinn, we would use the tags: Julia Quinn, regency romance, romance, romantic comedy, Duke & I. A handful of tags is all that is needed. In some places, Goodreads asks for Keywords. As far as we can figure, Keywords and Tags are used interchangeably on this site. In fact, when entering a review you are given the choice of Tags/Bookshelf. This allows you to choose the bookshelf that you have associated this book with as well as tags that will allow readers to find your review by searching tags/keywords. To play with this function, enter your favorite keyword/tag in various search fields and see what comes up. We played for a while using the Tag of 'Romance' and in some locations the word romance had to be in the search result. On other locations, the word 'Romance' seemed to be a true tag that someone had entered. As we go forward in our description of the various aspects of Goodreads, you will see how frequently you have the opportunity to use Tags and Keywords.

Chapter 13 — Author Profile

Every author needs to fill out an Author Application to create his or her Author Profile and gain all of the special functionality it brings.

Though similar to the Personal Profile, the Author Profile must be completed in addition to it. As you can see from the graphic above, fill in your author name, gender, date of birth, city of birth (if you choose), and copy and paste your official biography into the relevant box. Agree to the Terms & Conditions and then upload your photograph (see arrow above). Note that you should be using the same photo of yourself for reasons beyond the scope of this book.

To view how your information will appear, click on 'Home' on the main menu bar and look for a box that looks like the following:

Author Dashboard

The Author's Guide to Working With
Book Bloggers
20 people added it
13 ratings | 8 reviews

Visit your dashboard »

If you click on the green 'Visit your dashboard' link you will be taken to the following screen:

The Author Dashboard is your central reference point for your Author Platform. We will work our way through the various additions to the author profile. After you finish each step, go back to your Author Dashboard to ensure that each step is visible.

Chapter 14 — Link Your Blog Feed

The next step in the creation of your Author Profile is to add your blog feed. Although it is often overlooked, this simple step will garner more followers for your blog.

As you can see from the graphic above, click the 'Add a Blog' link to open the page that will allow you to do so.

The website lets you attach the feed of a pre-existing blog while also allowing you to have a Goodreads hosted one. We will start by hooking up your blog. As pictured in the graphic below, enter the feed URL for your blog and click 'Add Feed.'

If your feed was entered correctly, you should see the following:

If your latest blog post shows up as mine did (in the graphic above), you will have entered your feed URL correctly, and you can then click on the 'Save Changes' button. If you don't know your feed URL, either click on the RSS feed button on your blog or ask your blog designer for help. As a quick test, try to use http://yourdomain.com/feed/ as the feed. This is the most common feed url for blogs.

Adding your blog feed to your Author Profile at Goodreads is not only good for attracting new readers, but also beneficial from an SEO perspective. That topic is beyond the scope of this book, but let's just say it is good for your SEO.

Creating a Goodreads Hosted Blog Post

It is possible to post a Goodreads-hosted blog post. This functionality allows authors to add a quick note that is visible to site members, but not on their independent blog.

As you can see from the above graphic, there is a link at the bottom of the 'Your Blog' section that allows you to 'Write a New Post.' Click on it and the following screen will appear:

Enter the information you would like to appear and click 'Publish.' The resulting post will look like this:

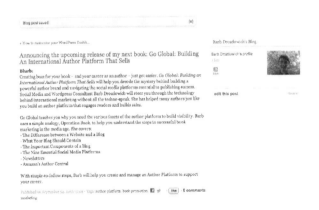

This post will appear with all your other blog posts on Goodreads, but will not appear on your independent blog.

53

Chapter 15 — Attach Your Book(s) to Your Profile

The next step is to make sure your titles are attached to your Author Profile. This might be unnecessary, as your books may already be associated with your profile, but if they aren't, this is what you need to do.

The first step is to search for your book. Enter your book title or ISBN and click 'Search.' If, as shown below, your book has not been added to Goodreads' database, you will have to import it manually (see arrow).

When you click on 'Manually Add a Book,' you will see the screen above. Fill in the form completely. Remember to add your cover image by using the button in the upper right-hand corner. When you are finished, click 'Save' at the bottom of the page.

The above page will appear next, allowing you to place your latest book on a shelf. We chose 'Read' and clicked on 'Save.'

If you return to your Author Dashboard, you will see your book in place (see graphic below).

Author Dashboard

Check the stats for your books and giveaways, and learn more about how to promote your books on Goodreads.

Barb Drozdowich's Stats

Barb Drozdowich's Stats

★★★★★ 4.86 avg rating — 7 ratings

number of works	2	added by unique users	9
total books added	10	fans	2
total ratings	7	friends	1,938
total reviews	3	books I've added	263
on to-read shelf	2	books I've reviewed	5

My Books

recent work stats

The Author's Guide to Working W...
by Barb Drozdowich
7 ratings (4.86 avg) · 3 text reviews
to-read: 2 people
currently-reading: 1 person

ebooks (1) | edit | stats

Go Global: Building an Internat...
by Barb Drozdowich
0 ratings (0.0 avg) · 0 text reviews

add ebook | edit | stats

rating & review stats are compiled from all editions of each work.

56

Chapter 16 — Posting Excerpts of Your Book

It is our experience that people love to read excerpts. Not only does it give them a feel for an author's writing style, but also it gives them a glimpse of the storyline. Most people put a lot of thought into the purchase of a novel. Just as you should have excerpts available on your blog, you should offer them on Goodreads. A large number of members purchase books directly from their Goodreads account after all!

Uploading an excerpt is a fairly straightforward process. Scroll down towards the bottom of your Author Dashboard and you will see the section depicted by the graphic below:

Click on the 'Add Ebook' link, as indicated by the arrow, and you will see the following screen:

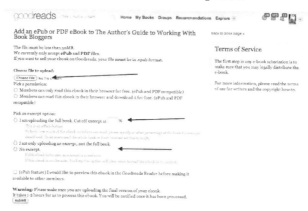

The excerpt file you upload must either be an ePub or PDF. To get the file from your hard drive, click on 'Choose File,' as indicated by the top arrow. Then 'pick a permission.' You can either allow members to read the excerpt on their browser or to read it on their browser and download it for free. You also need to indicate that what you are uploading is an excerpt. If you have uploaded the whole book then indicate where you want the excerpt cut off. Lastly, I suggest you choose to preview your excerpt before making it public to make sure it looks the way you want it to. Finally, click to 'Submit' your file.

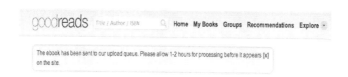

Once the file has been uploaded, the above confirmation screen will appear.

Chapter 17 — Video and Book Trailers

Adding videos or book trailers to your Goodreads account is easy to do, and another attractive feature for readers.

Videos may be added to any author profile as long as they are hosted on YouTube or the other services listed below. To add a video, click on 'Videos' on your author profile and then 'Add a New Video.' The following screen will appear.

Just follow the prompts to connect your latest book trailer. Keep in mind that videos can only be embedded from YouTube.com, Brightcove.com or Livestream.com. It is possible to add more than one video. It is generally accepted that the videos that are added are book trailers, but there is no reason you can't upload other videos associated with your Author career.

Chapter 18 — Author Widgets

As discussed earlier, Goodreads widgets should form an important part of your networking efforts with potential readers. Author widgets are a bit different from reader widgets in that they allow you to display reviews, and encourage people to read and rate your book. The graphic below shows how a Review Widget looks on a blog.

Goodreads offers a widget that you can attach to your cover graphic, which simply says 'Review this Book,' along with an 'Add My Books' widget and another one to show off your publications to potential readers. As with the reader widgets, once you submit the information you want shown, the code is supplied for insertion into your blog sidebar. Have a look at the selection and see if any of the choices interest you.

Chapter 19 — Goodreads Groups

Groups are a good way to introduce yourself to new readers and fans. There are quite a few authors' and readers' groups. They cover every genre and include people from many different countries. Some groups are focused on writing and some groups are focused on reading. This is where uber fans get to gush about books they love!

So, how do these groups work? With the restricted, private and secret groups, only members can view the discussion boards. In contrast, the discussion boards of public groups are available to all. For all groups, if you are a member you can add books to the group shelves or invite other members. Group administrators can remove members, delete discussion posts and add other moderators.

Certain groups are featured by Goodreads, whose editorial staff handpicks those highlighted in the 'Featured Groups' category. If you would like to nominate your group to be considered for inclusion, you can do it HERE. Please note that private groups are not eligible.

Now that we know what groups are, let's discuss how you can create one.

Create a Group

Click on 'Groups' in the header (marked in the graphic above) and then 'Create a Group' under the menu bar (see arrow). The following screen will appear:

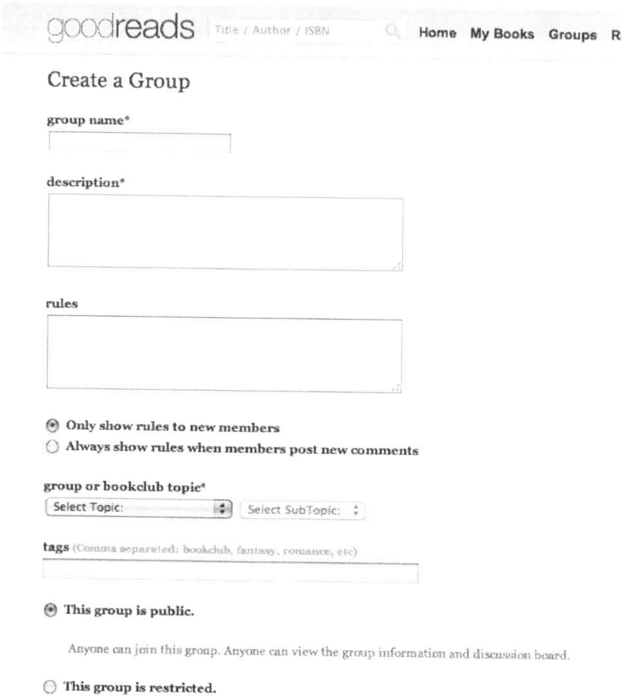

goodreads | Title / Author / ISBN   **Home**   **My Books**   **Groups**   R

Create a Group

group name*

description*

rules

◉ Only show rules to new members
◯ Always show rules when members post new comments

group or bookclub topic*

Select Topic: Select SubTopic:

tags (Comma separated: bookclub, fantasy, romance, etc)

◉ **This group is public.**

    Anyone can join this group. Anyone can view the group information and discussion board.

◯ **This group is restricted.**

To create the group, the fields above need to be filled in. Decide on a name for your group and write a few sentences of description about it. The next field will be 'Rules.' Every group needs at least basic rules – manners, etc. Put down a few sentences for now and refine them as time goes by. Although I would suggest only showing the rules to new members, you might choose to show them every time someone tries to post a comment. The next step is to choose the topic and, if applicable, a subtopic. Finally, you pick tags. All groups are searchable by name, but more importantly by tags, so choose these carefully.

As we have stated previously, there are several types of groups: public, which anyone can view and join; restricted, where anyone can see the information but only members can post to discussions; private, to which new members must be invited and approved by moderators, but anyone can see the content; and secret, where new members must be invited and approved by the moderators and only members can see information.

As the creator of a group, you need to decide who will be allowed to do various things, such as posting book covers. Ensure that you go though the list of choices and make the right selections for your new group.

So, the question is why should you create a group? There are pros and cons to this. One of the pros is that it will, potentially, allow you to interact with a large number of readers. Remember, if you create a group with the sole aim of selling your book, people will recognize this quickly and abandon it. Networking is the thing you should be aiming for.

At the top of the cons list is the amount of time required to promote and moderate a busy group. If you are trying to balance a full-time job, family and a writing career, as well as wanting to sleep at night, you might want to consider how much networking you could really accomplish with a group. We are not trying to discourage you here. We've seen groups done well and the potential is endless, but we know that we don't have the time to do a good job ourselves.

To turn off notifications, click on the group you wish to change. Where it says, 'You are a member,' click 'Edit group info,' and this will take you to a new page that resembles the screenshot below.

Topics I'm Following in Group

	get emails:	digest	individual	all	notification only	none
all topics within group		○	○	○	○	◉
Introduction (topic)		○	◉	○	○	○
Free Days (topic)		○	◉	○	○	○

As you can see, it is possible to modify what information you get from the group. If you don't appreciate your inbox being flooded with information, choose 'none' for all the topics.

Group Widgets

Every group has the ability to have a unique widget. Like reader widgets or author widgets that we have discussed above, these widgets are easy to create and easy to place on your blog sidebar to advertise your group. To find the Group Widgets, bring up the group you want a widget for, click on 'edit' beside the phrase 'You are a member.' (see arrow below)

Book Promo Central

A place were authors can come and get all the help they need in one place. Don't know how to do something? We can help.

You are a member. Edit | Group info

Part way down the next screen, you will see a 'Group Widget' section as seen in the graphic below. Choose what aspect of the group you want to advertise and then copy the code indicated by the arrow in the graphic below and past it into a text widget on your blog.

Group Widget

Add a widget to your blog or website that shows off your membership in this group.

To add a widget, please adjust your settings and cut and paste the HTML below on your website!

What your widget might look like.

This widget will not work on sites that don't allow javascript widgets (e.g. MySpace).

Chapter 20 — Post Group Activity to Facebook Page

If you decide to go ahead and create a Goodreads group, did you know that you can post its activity on Facebook? We'll outline below the steps that you need to take to do that.

Step one is to create a Facebook Fan Page for your group (if you don't already have one) as seen in the graphic below.

Create a corresponding Goodreads Group: (see screenshot below).

Connect Facebook to Goodreads by using the Goodreads Facebook App. To do this, type Goodreads into the search box on Facebook, as shown below.

Click on the gear (see arrow in above graphic).

When you click on the gear, a menu will drop down

Select 'Add App to Page' from the menu (see graphic above).

Choose the Facebook Page to which you would like to add Goodreads by using the drop down menu seen in the graphic above.

Navigate back to your Facebook Page and click on the Goodreads box near the top right.

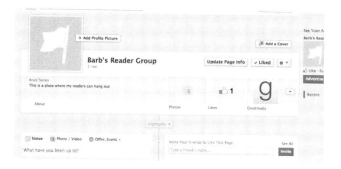

Lastly, select the type of 'Profile data' and choose one. Choose which Group Page you want associated with this Goodreads Group. You can only select those groups of which you are a moderator. Choose the group. Save and you're done. (see graphic below)

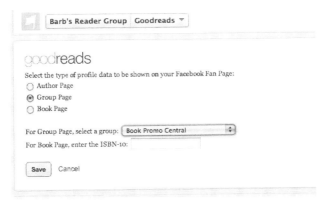

Chapter 21 — Q&A Discussion Group for Authors (Featured Author Group)

These are accessible towards the bottom of your Author Dashboard (see screenshot below). A Q&A group is a type of a featured author group.

Q&A Groups

Q&A groups are a way for authors to interact with readers and create buzz about their books. Authors form a group and agree to answer questions about their books for a brief period, and Goodreads will help promote the group using its word of mouth tools.

Read more on creating a Q&A group »

If you click on 'Read more' (above) you will reach the screen below.

Form a Featured Author Group to interact with readers

Featured Author Groups are a way for authors to interact with readers and create buzz about their books. Authors form a group and agree to answer questions about their books for a brief period, and Goodreads will help promote the group using its word of mouth tools.

How to Create a Featured Author Group

Sign up for our Authors Program, and make sure to add photos, videos, events, book excerpts, and a link to the featured group to your profile.

Create a special group "Ask [Author Name]" or "[Author Name] hosts a Q&A." Make sure to categorize it as a "Goodreads Author" group. The group description should clearly state what time range the author will be available to answer questions—we recommend running your group for a single day.

We recommend creating a single discussion topic called "Ask me something!" or something similar. This makes it easy for you, with just a single thread to check, and easy for your fans. To start the thread, write a post welcoming everyone to your group and asking for questions.

Goodreads will feature the group in the groups and authors sections of the site. Also, once a few people have joined the group, it will have the chance to spread virally and naturally though the Goodreads community.

Goodreads features several author Q&As in our monthly newsletter. To be considered for the newsletter, please contact us.

Create a Featured Author Group now »

Click on 'Create a Featured Author Group now' to reach the page shown below.

Next, fill in the 'Create a Group' form. The fields are fairly straightforward, and there are several choices that can be made with respect to rules and moderation. When you're done, scroll to the bottom and click 'Create.'

So, why should you create a Q&A group? The obvious answer is for networking. This sort of group will allow your friends and fans to ask you questions and engage you in dialogue, enabling you to get to know your readers better. The negative side is the time it requires. When organized properly, a Q&A group can enable you to create your own little Goodreads community. Like all communities, however, they require care and time. If this isn't something you could dedicate time to, you might want to think twice about starting.

One last word about Goodreads Groups. If you click on 'Groups' from the main menu and scroll part way down the screen, you will find the list of three 'Official Groups.' These are seen in the screenshot below. As their names suggest, one is called Goodreads Feedback and is designated for members to leave comments and suggestions. The second one is the Goodreads Librarians Group. The librarians know a lot on Goodreads and can answer almost any question. If you are stumped by something, post a question in this group and you will get an answer quite quickly.

The Goodreads Author Feedback Group is a good group to join if you are an author. We find the information that comes from this group quite helpful.

Official Groups

Goodreads Feedback

 13,977 members

Goodreads Librarians Group

 35,621 members

Goodreads Author Feedback Group

 4,286 members

Chapter 22 — Goodreads Events

Events are a popular feature on the website. They can be used to inform your friends of an online event, such as a blog tour, as well as an in-person event like a book signing. We will do a quick review that covers all aspects of this feature.

To find the events tool, click on 'Explore' on the top menu bar and look for Events. As you can see from the graphic below, it is at the bottom of the list.

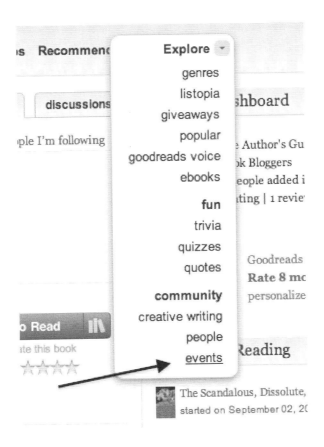

Clicking on this option will bring up the screen below, which will allow you to search all upcoming events.

Create an Event

To create an event, click on the 'Add an event' link on the right-hand side of the above screen.

As the name suggests, this page will allow you to add an event. As mentioned above, events can be used to let people know about any type of event, from book signings to cover reveals or giveaways on your blog. The form is basically set up

74

to create an in-person event such as a book signing, but if you are not organizing one of these, simply ignore irrelevant fields.

To create an event, enter the start and end dates, give it a name (be clear – Book release announcement for 'your book title' by 'your author name'), and enter a website that people can visit for more information. Goodreads is a networking place, so sending people to your blog for information about your event is a good plan, and a way of introducing them to your blog in the process. Unless the event is a physical one, skip the address information and go straight to the description. Make sure you leave your event as 'Public' (unless it is private and invitation-only), so that everyone can see it, and not only the people you invite. Once you're done, click 'Create' and your event will go live.

Invite People to an Event

The next step is to invite people. The following page appears automatically when you click on the 'Create' link:

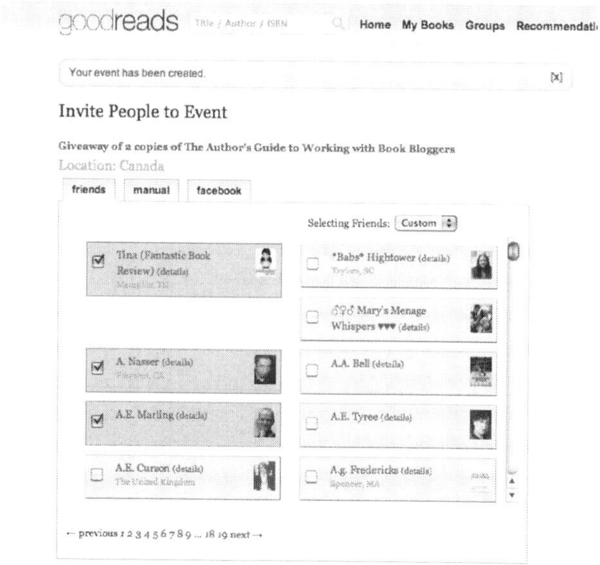

You can invite people by clicking the box by their name and then clicking on the 'Invite' box at the bottom of the page. We suggest inviting 200 at a time. Log out and log back in, and try to invite more. Generally speaking, creators of events should be able to invite 500 people each day, but we have heard of an author who can invite a lot more than that. Give it a try and see how many you can invite to your next event.

It is possible to see a list of events to which you have been invited (including your own) by clicking on 'My Events' on the right-hand side of the screen. You will then see the following graphic:

Upcoming Events for Barb Drozdowich (showing 1-13 of 13)

It is also possible to view 'All Events.' When you click on that link on the upper right-hand side of the screen, you will get a list of all public events. This is one good reason to create a public one – anyone searching through the events can find yours, even if they are not a friend.

Chapter 23 — Book Giveaways

Book giveaways are a wonderful way to get noticed. Remember that they are for paperbacks only at this time, although we hope this will change in the future. You should offer at least 25 copies before release and 25 afterwards. This is the best way to get your book noticed and on 'Want to read' lists. Goodreads claims the average giveaway attracts 825 entries and that more than 400,000 people enter them daily.

Posting a giveaway is easy. At the top of the Goodreads page, click on 'Explore' on the menu bar (see graphic below).

Next, choose 'Giveaways' – the third item from the top – which will take you to the page shown below.

Enter the appropriate information in the fields above. When choosing countries to ship to, keep in mind that this is for a paper book and you will be paying for shipping. When you are finished, click 'Save,' and you will receive a confirmation email from Goodreads. You need to respond to the confirmation notice for your giveaway to appear. This step is very important!

Chapter 24 — Reading Challenges

Reading challenges can be great for several reasons:

- Other readers/ fans can see what books you are reading
- Everyone else can see these books and add them to their own lists.

They are also another way for readers and fans to interact with their favorite authors. In the example shown below, Babs is working her way through her '2013 Reading Challenge Goal.'

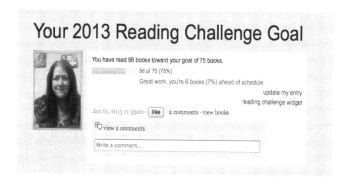

Challenges have the following important points:

- People can leave comments for you and ask about other books
- You can update your entry if you read faster or slower
- You can view your own list in order to track your progress

As you can see in the graphic below, Babs joined 413,661 other readers in the 2013 challenge. Wouldn't it be great to be part of a group of 413,661 readers? Great networking potential!

You can place a Reading Challenge widget on your blog if you like. These gadgets are found by going to your Profile, choosing 'Edit' and clicking on 'Widgets.' The image below shows how they look.

Authors who join in the challenge are not only helping themselves, but other authors as well. You will be promoting the books you are reading. When other members see your list they will be more likely to add these books to their own shelves. Remember, you want your books to be added to their 'To-read' shelf to help its rankings.

81

Chapter 25 — Recommend Books

To get your book noticed, you should recommend it to your friend and fan lists.

One of the main points you need to be aware of on Goodreads, as well as all other social media sites, is that being blatantly self-promotional all the time will be tuned out by most users. Therefore, don't immediately recommend *your* book to others. This should be part of a larger communication strategy. To start with, recommend some of your favorite novels.

The image below shows what your page will look like when you click 'Home' followed by 'Recommendations.' As you can see, you can choose to put a recommended book on one of your shelves or choose "not interested". There are more options on the right-hand side of the graphic below.

This screenshot shows what Babs' recommendations are. Check to see what books are recommended for you.

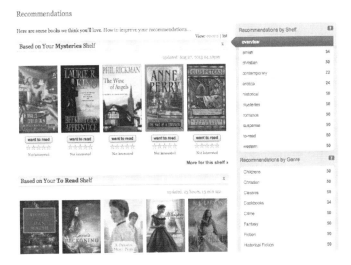

To improve your recommendations, do the following:

- Rate more books, because the more you rate, the better the results will be. In order to get accurate recommendations, you need to rate at least 20

- Update your favorite genres (be specific and limited)

- Categorize the books you have listed by creating shelves such as science fiction or history. Goodreads makes recommendations based on the shelves you create

- Click 'Not interested' on the recommendations you don't like. That way, Goodreads will be less likely to show you similar books in future.

Chapter 26 — Listopia

Goodreads uses Listopia, of which everyone – authors as well as readers – should take advantage. You can create your own list and have people vote on the books on it, which is a good way to get noticed and network. The lists are all public, so everyone can view the ones they find interesting.

To make a list you will need to click 'Explore' on the top bar to view the drop menu. As you can see from the screenshot below, Listopia is the second entry.

Clicking on 'Listopia' will take you to the page below.

To create your own list, click on 'Create a list' in the upper right-hand corner.

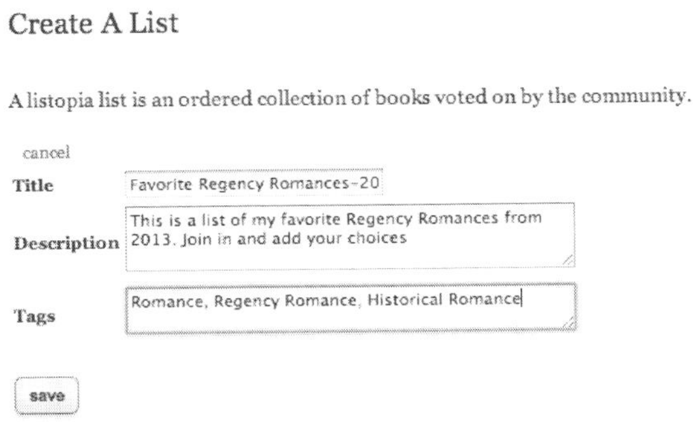

Create A List

A listopia list is an ordered collection of books voted on by the community.

cancel

Title	Favorite Regency Romances-20
Description	This is a list of my favorite Regency Romances from 2013. Join in and add your choices
Tags	Romance, Regency Romance, Historical Romance

save

The screen above shows a list that we created with the title of Favorite Regency Romances – 2013. You can see that we filled in a description and added some appropriate tags. When you click on the 'Save' button you will be brought to the next screen where you can add books to this list. (see arrow below) Make sure you click on 'Update' before you leave this screen. Check back in periodically to see who has voted on your list and if any comments have been added. Not only is it great to have your books added to lists, but this has great networking potential with readers!

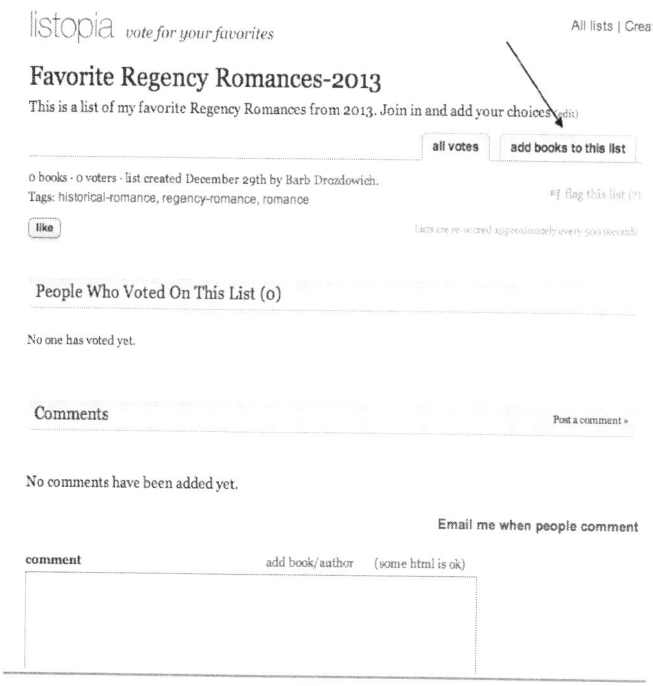

listopia *vote for your favorites*

All lists | Crea

Favorite Regency Romances-2013

This is a list of my favorite Regency Romances from 2013. Join in and add your choices (edit)

| all votes | add books to this list |

0 books · 0 voters · list created December 29th by Barb Drozdowich.
Tags: historical-romance, regency-romance, romance

⚑ flag this list (?)

[like]

Lists are re-scored approximately every 500 seconds

People Who Voted On This List (0)

No one has voted yet.

Comments

Post a comment »

No comments have been added yet.

Email me when people comment

comment   add book/author   (some html is ok)

Chapter 27 — Trivia

Trivia is a good way of getting your readers more involved with your books. Create at least one question for each title to engage your fans.

To make one, go to the top menu bar and click 'Explore'. Then click 'Trivia' on the dropdown menu. To add a new question, click on the 'Add a question' indicated by the arrow in the graphic below.

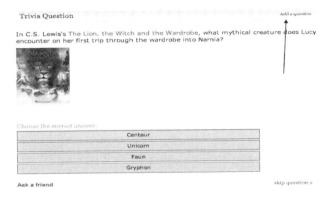

You will be taken to a new page (see below). Filling it in is fairly straightforward. We suggest creating questions from the content of your books. Don't make the questions too difficult, but centered on key plot points of your work.

Create a Trivia Question

When you have finished creating a question, click on the 'create question' button and your question will be added to the selection that people can answer.

When readers answer trivia questions, they can find out if their answer is correct, whether or not others thought it was a good question, and whether or not their friends got the question correct. The example below shows the response to a question about Beverly Cleary's work.

Last Question (answered 282181 times)   Recent

In Beverly Cleary's popular kids' books, what is Beezus's real name?

You got it right!

a. Ramona 43583 (18.9%)

b. Rebecca 10230 (4.4%)

c. Beatrice 170191 (74.0%)*

d. Sabrina 6016 (2.6%)

ask a friend | details

rate this question

Was this a good question?   yes   no
75.1% out of 754 people liked it.

Take Other Questions About

Author:

Beverly Cleary

Friends Responses

Nely Sanchez got it right.
Ned Hayes got it wrong.
Jackie Burris got it right.
Nikki Brandyberry got it right.
Louisa Klein got it wrong.
Suzie Quint skipped it.
Bonnie skipped it.
Elisabeth Wheatley skipped it.
Brian Anderson got it right.
Melodie Ramone got it right.

Chapter 28 — Quizzes

Quizzes are just as useful for connecting with readers. Every author should plan to create a series of quiz questions for each of their books. To find the Quiz section, click on 'Explore' on the main menu and click on 'Quiz' near the bottom of the list. As you can see in the graphic below, there is quite a wide variety of Quizzes available. Goodreads sorts the quizzes into various categories and they can also be searched by tag. Some of these quizzes are taken by many readers. Looking at the graphic below, you'll notice that the Hunger Games quiz has been taken almost half a million times!

You may notice below that it is possible to create quiz questions about authors, books as well as just general questions. As an author, you can create quiz questions about yourself, but our main focus is creating questions about books. Below are some screenshots of the process from the start.

Create a Quiz

Quiz Guidelines

quiz title*

quiz description

add book/author

tags (separated by a comma)

- Please avoid spoilers in your quiz description and first question.
- Only add literary-related questions.
- Please use the "add book/author" links when mentioning which books and authors the question is about. This will ensure the question appears on the correct book and author pages on the site.
- Please don't add personal questions — quizzes are for everyone, not just your friends.
- Offensive language or images will be removed.

Suggestions

Image (optional)

Choose File   no file selected

this quiz is about

Fill this out correctly to improve browsing and the photo associated with this quiz.

- General
- Author
- Book

Make this quiz visible in the quiz index
(book and author related quizzes only)

question 1

add book/author

- General
- Author
- Book

Make this quiz visible in the quiz index
(book and author related quizzes only)

question 1

add book/author

answer 1   correct:

answer 2   correct:

answer 3   correct:

answer 4   correct:

add answer | remove answer

question 2

add book/author

answer 1   correct:

answer 2   correct:

answer 3   correct:

As you can see from the graphics above, the quiz questions that you are creating are multiple choice which allows readers to easily guess if they aren't certain. You can add as many questions as you like. Authors who are experienced with Goodreads have mentioned how some readers prefer quizzes while others love trivia, so they run both to capture all readers.

By creating a quiz or some trivia questions, you can challenge your readers to find them on Goodreads and complete them to be entered into a draw, or to win some sort of a prize. You don't have to wait to see if anyone discovers your questions. You can send them in the right direction.

Chapter 29 — Creative Writing

As authors, one thing we love about Goodreads is that we can post creative writing on our profile. This is another great way of interacting with your fans. These people are naturally drawn to your writing, so why not share some?

To do this, go to the menu bar and click on 'Explore.' The dropdown box will show 'Creative Writing' under 'Community' (see graphic below).

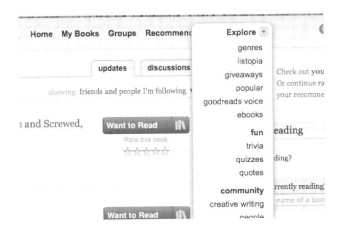

Clicking on 'Creative writing' will bring up another page (see graphic below) where you will see some creative writing samples subdivided according to genre, most active, popular, written by friends and new entries. Before you enter your own work, browse the selections already added and see what others have chosen to share.

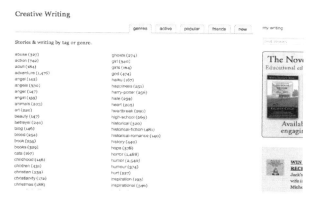

To enter your creative writing sample, click on the 'My writing' link, top right. This will take you to a new page where you can start writing. Below are screenshots of the things you will need to fill out to get started.

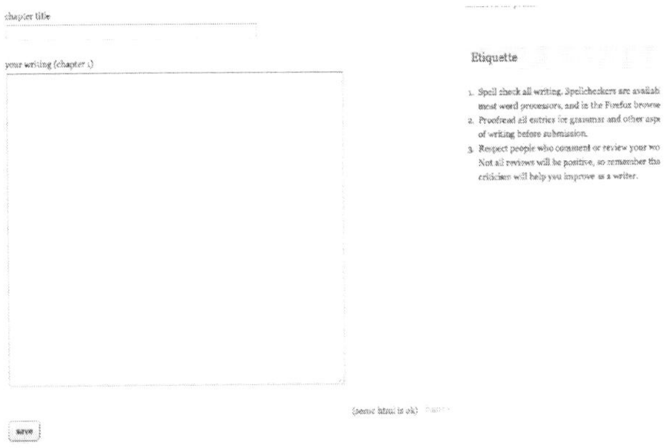

When entering information in the page depicted above, ensure that you choose the appropriate genre and a selection of tags are used to help others find your work. To help find tags, consider looking at the selection of popular tags. (see graphic below)

Browse By Tag

| Search for a Tag | **Search** |

action (791)

adventure (1539)

death (1594)

drama (1464)

family (940)

fantasy (3767)

fiction (4002)

friendship (979)

horror (1556)

humor (2625)

life (1711)

love (4831)

magic (941)

murder (634)

mystery (1720)

paranormal (884)

poem (1101)

poetry (8350)

romance (7741)

sad (599)

science-fiction (1527)

short-story (1825)

story (631)

suspense (945)

teen (587)

thriller (1174)

vampires (657)

war (627)

writing (597)

young-adult (1069)

More...

Once you've completed a chapter, if you want to add another, click 'Edit/Add Chapter' (lower right-hand side of the image below).

Not only can readers vote to like various creative writing efforts, they can also comment. Creative writing is a great way to share with everyone from the aspiring author to the seasoned one.

Chapter 30 — Quotes

Submitting memorable quotes from your book is a commonly overlooked function of Goodreads. It is a simple, yet powerful addition to your networking efforts. To find the correct area in which to enter them, start from your 'Home' screen and click 'Explore' on the menu bar. You will see 'Quotes' towards the bottom of the list (shown by an arrow on the screenshot below).

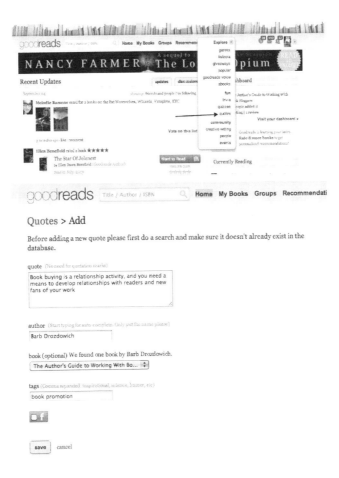

Simply fill out the above form and click on 'Save' to add a memorable quote from your work. As you are instructed on the screen, ensure that your quote hasn't been added by anyone else.

Ensure that appropriate tags are used. Although they are referred to as tags in the form, when searching, the same item is referred to as a keyword.

Chapter 31 — Polls

Polls are a great way for an author to find out more about readers. If you go to your 'home' page and scroll all the way down to the bottom, you will find 'Featured Poll' on the right-hand side (see graphic below)

Featured Poll

EReader users: do you highlight?
- ◯ Yes, I like to highlight
- ◯ No, I never highlight.
- ◯ I don't have an ereader
- ◯ my ereader doesn't support highlighting.
- ◯ other

next poll »

As you can see from the graphic above, Goodreads gives you the opportunity to answer a poll. These poll questions are generalized poll questions. The Polls that we will describe in this section are the ones that are created as a function of a group. If you have decided to take the leap and create your own group – perhaps a Q&A group or simply a group of like-minded readers, you can poll the group members by creating a poll question. To find the graphic below, bring up the group that you want to poll, and on the right side, one of the choices is 'Polls.'

Group Home	Events	Invite People
Bookshelf	Photos	Members
Discussions	Videos	Polls
Settings		

When you click on 'Polls' the following graphic will appear:

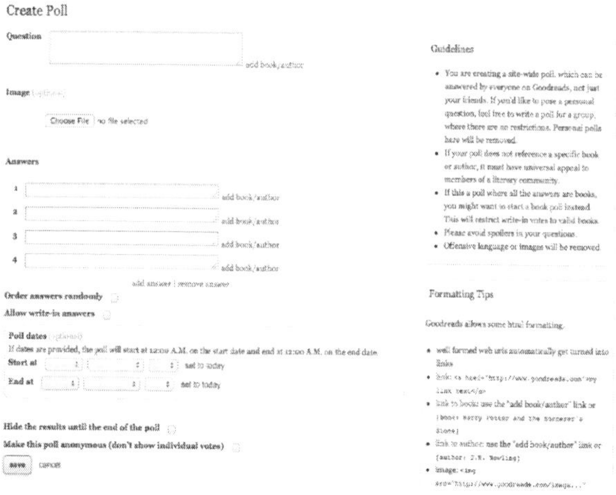

As you can see above, an image can be added to the poll and the answers can either be predetermined or free-format. The poll can have a start and an end date and the results can be hidden from the readers responding to the poll.

We feel that this is a great way of gathering information from readers. As in the Quiz and Trivia sections, if you have created a group, consider creating a poll and then inviting group members to complete the poll. See what you can learn.

Chapter 32 — Goodreads Advertising

Some authors believe adverts are a good feature while others are not so enthusiastic. It depends on the genre of your book and what is popular at the time. The setup for the Goodreads self-service advertising is quite simple and the ads do not have to be expensive.

According to Goodreads, your new ad will give you exposure to "an audience of more than 21 million book lovers. With more than 140 million page views and 19 million unique visitors a month, Goodreads offers advertisers integrated advertising and promotional programs to reach their highly affluent and educated audience of book readers". (from Goodreads help pages)

The easiest way to find the advertising options is to click on the 'down' arrow beside your profile picture and click 'Help' (see image below).

Or, if you start on your Author Dashboard, the link is near the bottom.

After clicking 'Help,' you will be taken to the page shown below. Click on 'Advertisers' on the left-hand side.

Goodreads Help Topics

About Goodreads

Jobs   **Search Help**   What do you want help with?

Blog

Press   my books

Contact   • How do I add a book to "my books"?

              • Can I edit a shelf for multiple books at once?

Advertisers   • Why are my status updates calculated in percents?

Author Program   • How do I create a "Never Finished" or "Abandoned" shelf?

              • How do I update my progress in a book I'm "currently reading"?

API   • How do I move a book from "currently reading" to "read"?

This will take you to another page about advertising on Goodreads. We recommend that you read this carefully to see if this option is for you.

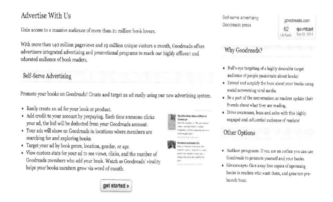

If you would like to go ahead, click on 'Self-Service Advertising' in the upper right-hand corner (shown above), which will take you to the 'Create an Ad' page (below).

First, give your advert or as Goodreads calls it, your campaign, a name. This title, as well as the Ad Name (next field) will only be visible to you. Decide on the type of ad you are creating, and then enter the ISBN or ASIN of your book, and click 'Load.'

As you can see from the screenshot above, once you click 'Load,' the page expands to allow you to enter the Ad Title, Ad Description, Destination URL, and the image that will be associated with it. Clicking 'Save' again will take you to

103

another screen where you can set a budget for your campaign and complete your order.

As you go through these pages, you will notice that 'Help' is always available at the right-hand side of the screen.

Finally, we have added two screenshots below regarding Goodreads' advertising guidelines, so you can acquaint yourself with them. Although we have heard many positive and negative responses to Goodreads advertising, we believe that you need to try it out for yourself. Barb currently has an advertisement in progress for her books, and although there haven't been many clicks, there have been thousands and thousands of impressions. In the Goodreads system, impressions are free.

Goodreads Advertising Creative Guidelines and Policies

About Advertising on Goodreads

Goodreads believes in empowering readers and creating a quality user experience, and this philosophy is embedded in the Goodreads design and all our features. We believe advertising on Goodreads should conform to this philosophy, and be a quality experience for our users.

The following guidelines are provided to help you construct quality ads to better engage with the Goodreads community. All advertising on Goodreads must adhere to these guidelines, and Goodreads reserves the right to reject anything that in our opinion does not adhere to our terms and philosophy.

Accounts:
- Advertisers are not permitted to manage multiple online advertising accounts.
- Advertisers must not programmatically automate the creation of accounts or ads.

Advertisements may not mislead the user:
- Free Offers must include simple access to all information pertaining to the method of qualifying for the Free Offer within the creative itself.
- Advertiser messaging must not promote false dietary claims or mislead consumers as noted by the Federal Trade Commission.
- All offers must comply with FTC guidelines and policies, and must not be deceptive, unfair, or contain deceptive pricing.
- Not Allowed: Advertising that constitutes bait and switch advertising pursuant to FTC guidelines.
- Not Allowed: Images without borders.

Software Downloads:
- Users must be informed as to exactly what is being offered for download.
- Not Allowed: Automatic Downloads or Download Command Boxes.
- Not Allowed: Hidden or harmful functionality as bundled components of a user approved download. Eg: software classified as AdWare/Spyware.
- Not Allowed: Ads that spawn Active X controls.

Adult Content:
- Bathing wear and undergarment advertising must be reviewed prior to acceptance.
- Pharmaceutical advertising promoting adult-oriented drugs must be approved prior to acceptance.
- Not Allowed: Nudity & sexually explicit images or content.
- Not Allowed: Provocative.

Sensitive Content:
- Religious content or advertising must be approved prior to acceptance.
- Political content or advertising must be approved prior to acceptance.
- Distracting or suggestive content must be approved prior to acceptance.
- Not Allowed: Advertising that promotes illegal activities or offers.
- Not Allowed: Advertising directed to children 13 years of age or younger.
- Not Allowed: Advertising that promotes discrimination, violence, or displays defamatory, profane, hateful, or libelous material.
- Not Allowed: Advertising that misrepresents, ridicules, or attacks an individual or group on the basis of age, color, national origin, race, religion, sex, sexual orientation or disability.
- Not Allowed: Anything that might trigger a serious phobia – eg. realistic spiders, cockroaches, snakes.

User Experience / Ad Functionality:
- Animation with standard advertising placements is limited to 15 seconds.
- Advertising creative that employs flashing, shaking, rolling, pulsing (etc.) must be approved prior to acceptance.
- Not Allowed: Blocking or impeding browser functionality from working as intended. "Back" button must work.
- Not Allowed: Advertising that features false system messaging, error messaging, dialog boxes, etc.
- Not Allowed: False application, system update, or diagnostic messaging.
- Not Allowed: False "Close", "Minimize", "Maximize", or other window functionality.
- Not Allowed: Advertising that mimics website design, functionality, navigation, service, or messaging.
- User-initiated audio that contains questionable language (swearing/sexual oriented).
- Not Allowed: Any Pops.

Chapter 33 — Goodreads Voice

The *Goodreads Voice* is Goodreads version of a reader magazine. It can be accessed under the 'Explore' menu, as shown by the graphic below.

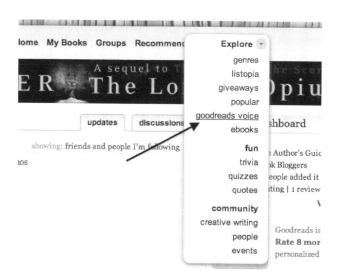

Once opened, *Goodreads Voice* displays author interviews, new books, videos, blog posts and a variety of other things. What isn't so well known is that you can request to be interviewed. Who is chosen is an editorial decision, but you can't be interviewed unless you ask. The *Goodreads Voice* is pictured in the screenshot below.

To request an interview, you will need to use the contact form. To find it, quickly, click on the down arrow by your avatar and choose help. The 'contact' link is the 5th link down on the right side.

Clicking it will produce the contact form as seen below.

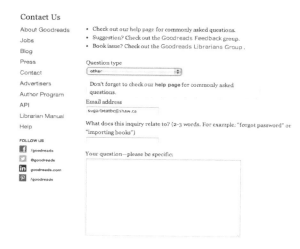

For 'Question Type,' we recommend choosing the category of 'Other' and filling out the appropriate information. When completed, click 'Send.

So, why would you want to apply to be included in the *Goodreads Voice*? Free exposure, of course! Although not everyone who requests an interview will appear on the newsletter, the networking potential is huge! Remember millions of eyes will read the *Goodreads Voice*.

Chapter 34 — Goodreads Author-focused Newsletter

Goodreads has an author newsletter, which goes out periodically. Unlike the general newsletter, it is not sent on a regular basis, but it contains some useful information. You will find some great marketing tips, ideas for promotion on Goodreads and website shortcuts. Although any author can subscribe to the ezine, in order to be included in the content, you will need to contact the website directly.

Goodreads' Newsletters

Goodreads sends out two general newsletters: one general and the other for YA. These are great for advertising opportunities. To be included or considered for advertising, contact Goodreads directly via the Contact Page.

Conclusion

We hope that you have enjoyed reading ***The Ultimate Goodreads Guide for Authors***. We realize that this book has a lot of information to absorb and to put into practice.

Goodreads is one of the best places on the Internet to have your book noticed, reviewed and accepted by millions of readers. There are many things on offer, which you, as an author, should take full advantage of. As with any product, there will be some aspects you love and others that are not for you, but, overall, if you give Goodreads a try, you will not be disappointed.

Try some of the functionality that is new to you. Drop us a note and let us know what you liked and what you didn't like about Goodreads. Or just drop us a note and let us know what you thought about our book!

Thank you for reading ***The Ultimate Goodreads Guide for Authors***! We hope you enjoyed it. If you did, please help other readers find this book by writing a review on the retail site you purchased this copy from.

Thank you for your support of our books! We so appreciate it!

About the Authors

Barb Drozdowich

Bio: Social Media and Wordpress Consultant Barb Drozdowich has taught at Colleges and Universities, trained technical personnel in the banking industry and, most recently, used her expertise to help dozens of authors develop the social media platform needed to succeed in today's fast evolving publishing world. She owns Bakerview Consulting and manages the popular Romance Book blog, Sugarbeat's Books.

Barb can be found:

Bakerview Consulting (Business Site) http://bakerviewconsulting.com

Barb Drozdowich (Author Site) http://barbdrozdowich.com

Sugarbeat's Books (Book Blog) http://sugarbeatsbooks.com

Facebook(Author blog) https://www.facebook.com/BarbDrozdowichAuthor

Twitter http://twitter.com/sugarbeatbc

Google+ https://plus.google.com/110824499539694941768

Book #1 in the Building Blocks to Author Success Series:

The Author's Guide to Working with Book Bloggers

Blurb:

Do you feel out of your comfort zone when dealing with book bloggers?

If Book Bloggers are the new gatekeepers to 'book publishing success' how can you tap into that source of free promotions? How can you move comfortably into that world, putting your best foot forward?

The Author's Guide to Working with Book Bloggers combines the advice of 215 bloggers covering all aspects of communication between authors and Review Blogs. Whether you are a new author, or have many titles under your belt, let us demystify the promotion of your book on a book blog.

You'll learn about whom and where book bloggers are, as well as the following:

- The Query
- The Review
- The Giveaway
- The Guest Post
- The Book Blurb Excerpt and Cover Reveals and more!

>>> Start your journey to publishing success today!

ISBN: 978-0-9898523-0-2

Book #2 in the Building Blocks to Author Success Series:

What's Your Author Platform? Create It, Understand It, Build It

Blurb:

Creating buzz for your book and your career as an author just got easier.

'What's Your Platform?' will help you create, understand and use a powerful author platform to sell books!

Social Media and Wordpress Consultant Barb Drozdowich will steer you through the technology behind book marketing without all the techno-speak. She has helped many authors just like you build an author platform that engages readers and builds sales.

This book will help you decode the mystery behind building a powerful author brand and navigating the social media platforms essential to publishing success.

'What's Your Platform?' teaches you why you need the various facets of the author platform to build visibility. Barb uses a simple analogy, Operation Book, to help you understand the steps to successful book marketing in the media age. She covers:

The Difference between a Website and a Blog

The Important Items Your Blog Should Contain

The Nine Essential Social Media Platforms

Newsletters

Amazon's Author Central and many more

>>> **With simple-to-follow steps, Barb will help you create, understand and use an Author Platform to support your career.**

ISBN: 978-0-9898523-2-6

Book #3 in the Building Blocks to Author Success Series:

Book Blog Tours – An Essential Marketing Tool for Authors

Blurb:

What's your verdict on Book Blog Tours?
Great idea....or a waste of time and money?

Not sure what a book blog tour can do for your visibility as an author or the promotion of your book? Are you considering trying out a Book Blog Tour to market your newest release? Do you want a primer that will help you take confident steps into the book promotion world? Why not learn about Book Blog Tours from the point of view of a Blogger and a Reader?

Book Blog Tours covers topics such as:

- How to set goals for a blog tour
- Look at Giveaways from the point of view of a blogger and a reader

Babs Hightower

Bio: Babs has been helping authors since 2000. She owns a book review blog Babs Book Bistro which got her started in PR and helping authors promote themselves. In 2012 she started working for Entangled Publishing and worked her way up to Publicity Director over the Scandalous Imprint. She is a publicist for World Castle Publishing. She is also known as Morgan Kincaid writer of Historical Romance.

Babs can be found:

Babs Book Bistro website: http://www.babsbookbistro.net

Babs Hightower PR website: http://www.babshightowerpr.com

Author website: http://morgankincaid.com

Twitter: https://twitter.com/babsbookbistro

Twitter: https://twitter.com/BabsMorganKin

Facebook: https://www.facebook.com/BabsHightowerPr

Facebook Author: https://www.facebook.com/authormorgankincaid

LinkedIn: www.linkedin.com/in/babsbookbistro/

Goodreads: http://www.goodreads.com/user/show/1970552-babs

Google +: https://plus.google.com/u/0/102563748897854093407/posts

Pinterest: http://www.pinterest.com/babsbookbistro

Book #1 Public Relations for Authors Take Hold of Your Own Promotions

Blurb:

Getting help to promote your book just got easier. Public Relations for Authors Take Hold of Your Own Promotions will help you locate that special publicist who will help you promote your book the right way. A Publicity Director for two publishers Babs brings knowledge to this book.

Public Relations teach you why you need a publicist and how to find the right one for you. To understand what you need she covers:

- How publicity can help sell books

- What you need to know about publicity

- Writing Pitches

- Media Kits

- Press Releases

- Where to find a PR agent

- What to send to your PR agent

ISBN: 978-0-9898523-1-9

Made in the USA
San Bernardino, CA
26 October 2014